At the Fire Station

by Victor Violi

PEARSON

Glenview, Illinois • Boston, Massachusetts • Chandler, Arizona
Upper Saddle River, New Jersey

Firefighters fight a fire!
They work as a team.
Each firefighter has a job.
Some firefighters drive the truck.

Firefighters use a hose.
They spray water on the fire.
Firefighters wear helmets.
They also wear masks.
Helmets and masks help firefighters
stay safe.

Even firefighters have to study.

On some days, firefighters
take classes.
They learn to use new tools.

Firefighters teach children.

Some firefighters visit schools.
They tell children about fires.
Firefighters teach children how
to stay safe.

Firefighters wash the trucks.

Most firefighters stay at the station
day and night.
They sleep there.
Firefighters work at the station too.
They keep it clean.

Everyone helps at the station.

Firefighters eat at the station.
Some buy and cook food.
Others wash the dishes.

Firefighters use poles to
move fast.

The alarm rings. Fire!
Firefighters hurry to fight the fire.
They are very busy.